Essays Towards Restoring the African Mind

Dwayne Wong (Omowale)

CONTENTS

1 THE STRUGGLE OVER AFRICAN HISTORY

The European assault on African people was a brutal one. During slavery, colonization, Jim Crow, apartheid, and all of the other systematic forms of racism and oppression African people were brutalized, raped, lynched, burned alive, buried alive, castrated, beheaded, whipped, mutilated, and suffered many other forms of physical violence. What also went into this oppression was the stripping of the very identity of African people through the robbing of their history. On the slave plantations African people were stripped of their languages, names, cultural practices, and religion. Those Africans who attempted to maintain their language or culture were brutally punished. Olaudah Equiano recalled that he was renamed Gustavus Vassa and when he refused to acknowledge his new name he was beaten until he submitted.

Africans were forced to adjust to a society that was hostile and contrary to the society that they knew. Whereas African societies tended to be family orientated, life for Africans on the slave plantations was the opposite. Husbands and wives, parents and children, grandparents and grand-children, were all separated from each other on a regular basis. Therefore, the very lifestyles of African people were altered on the slave plantations. This contributed to the fracturing of the identities of African people.

Robbing African people of their sense of self served two major purposes. One of which was making African more docile and less rebellious. This was so effective that many Africans refused to run away from the plantations even when given the opportunity to do so. Harriet Tubman often carried a pistol with her not only for self-defense, but to threaten those who wanted to return to the plantations after having left. The other purpose of this robbing of the self-identity of African people was that by reinforcing this idea that African people were an inferior and savage people with no history Europeans also justified their own mistreatment of African people.

The erasing of history played a critical role in approaches to the academic study of African history, especially as it related to Egypt. Marcus Garvey (1923) pointed out that white historians flat out denied the racial identity of the Egyptians:

The white world has always tried to rob and

discredit us of our history. They tell us that Tut-Ankh-Amen, a King of Egypt, who reigned about the year 1350 B. C. (before Christ), was not a Negro, that the ancient civilization of Egypt and the Pharaohs was not of our race, but that does not make the truth unreal.

Garvey's statement should be elaborated on a bit more given the fact that the debate over the identity of the Egyptians best exemplifies the extent that Western scholars have gone to discredit African history or to deny African people their rightful place in history. It should be made clear from the onset that a very popular tactic used to discredit African history has been to ascribe any achievements in Africa to outside influences. For example, in Rhodesia the government took the position that the ruins of Great Zimbabwe were built by non-African people and any information that proved otherwise was suppressed. W.E.B. Du Bois (1915) dismissed the idea that the culture of West Africa was anything but native when he writes:

> Effort has naturally been made to ascribe this civilization to white people. First it was ascribed to Portuguese influence, but much of it is evidently older than the Portuguese discovery, Egypt and India have been evoked and Greece and Carthage. But all these explanations are far-fetched. If ever a people exhibited unanswerable evidence of

indigenous civilization, it is the west-coast Africans. Undoubtedly they adapted much that came to them, utilized new ideas, and grew from contact. But their art and culture is Negro through and through.

This idea of robbing African people of our history has also been part of the ongoing battle over who the Egyptians were. Egyptology arose during a time when the general perception was that African people were inferior and could not produce an empire such as Egypt—in fact, many European historians argued that African people made no contributions to world history or civilization. These scholars also believed that Africans could not have produced the Kushite/Nubian civilization. Nubia was usually explained away in two ways. Either Nubia was relegated to being a mere vassal state of Egypt which stole its civilization from Egypt or the Nubians were really white people. The latter view was the one taken up by Archibald Henry Sayce, who said of the Nubians: "These kings, like the court which surrounded them, belonged to the white race." This idea of Egyptians being white was so prevalent among Western scholars that when confronted with an Egyptian statue that resembled an African, Sir Flinders W. M. Petrie was left to assert that Sneferu's queen, Mertitefs, "might be of an inferior race and not of the 'high type.'"

Various writers have observed the similarities between the Egyptians and other African societies. Du Bois wrote that: "The evidence of language also connects Egypt with Africa and the Negro race rather than with Asia, while religious ceremonies and social customs all go to strengthen this evidence." He also pointed out that: "Many things show the connection between Egypt and this part of Africa. The same glass beads are found in Uganda and Upper Egypt, and similar canoes are built. Harps and other instruments bear great resemblance." E.A. Wallis Budge (1911) observed that many of the religious practices of the Egyptians were observed in many parts of Africa. Budge explains: "The ancient Egyptian, like the modern African, made offerings to the spirits of his ancestors with the view of keeping their help and protection by maintaining their existence, and he also did so in order to prevent them from being obliged to eat filth and drink polluted water."

Budge concluded from his trips to the Sudan:

> During subsequent visits to the Sudan I became convinced that a satisfactory explanation of the ancient Egyptian Religion could only be obtained from the Religions of the Sudan, more especially those of the peoples who lived in the isolated districts in the south and west of that region, where European influence was limited, and where native beliefs and religious ceremonials still possessed life and meaning.

The Haitian historian and anthropologist Anténor Firmin (1885) explained that "the existence of certain ceremonies and the preservation of certain symbols and signs in various African cultures are best explained in connection with the traditions or surviving practices from ancient Egypt." He continues on to note that "King Munsa of the Monbouttous is shown seated on his throne and holding the *harpe*, which is the same symbol of kingship and divine power among ancient Egyptians with which the Pharaohs are often represented."

Firmin also argued that conflicts between the Nubians (Ethiopians) and Egyptians was a "family affair." He explains: "They made alliances, they separated, they fought against one another, but they always united in difficult times." Firmin used the union between Nubia and Egypt as further proof of the argument that Egyptian civilization was an African civilization.

The 18th dynasty was perhaps Egypt's most prosperous dynasty, and it produced some of the most well-known figures in Egyptian history. This dynasty, based on the physical appearances of its rulers, was also one of the blackest dynasties. Egyptologist John Wilkinson (1883) stated of the features of Amenhotep III: "The features of this monarch cannot fail to strike every one who examines the portraits of the Egyptian kings, having more in common with the negro than those of any other Pharaoh; but it is difficult to say whether it was accidental, or in consequence of his mother having been of Ethiopian origin." Given Egypt's close connection to Nubia the second scenario is most likely. Moreover, it is worth pointing out that at various points in Egypt's history we find pharaohs from Nubia ruling in Egypt. The entire 25th dynasty was a Nubian one and pharaoh Amenemhat I of the 12th dynasty had a Nubian mother. Even Greek writers commented on the dark appearances of the Egyptians. For example, Herodotus wrote: "I believe that the Colchis are a colony of Egyptians because, like the latter, they have a black skin and woolly hair."

The issue of Egypt is related to the larger debate over African history and the attempts that have been made to suppress that history. The fact is that Western scholars have not been ignorant about African history, but have instead chosen to deny it or attempted to suppress such information. Historian William Leo Hansberry experienced this at Howard University when he attempted to introduce African history into the curriculum. He was met with resistance from some of the faculty. Two of Howard's most distinguished professors reported to the president of Howard—a white man named J. Stanley Durkee—that Hansberry was "endangering the standards and reputation of the university by teaching matters for which there is no foundation in fact." Based on this report, the president and the board of trustees voted to discontinue Hansberry's program. They later reversed their decision, but Hansberry no longer had the support of Durkee. Hansberry distinguished himself as one of the foremost experts on the subject of African history, but despite his thorough research and knowledge of the topic he was never given the respect and recognition from Howard

University that he deserved.

The issue of African history goes deeper than the academic aspect which has been abovementioned. History also plays a significant role in the very ability of African people to function properly. Amos Wilson (1993) explained, "We, as individuals, are our history." He states:

> If you forgot your past you would not be able to understand me right now. You would not be able to walk or talk. You did not learn to walk, and talk and do the things you're doing at the moment when you entered here; you learned to them in the past.

The repression of history also creates what Wilson terms "historical and experiential amnesia." This is to say that history contains problem solving abilities and the loss of that history creates a loss of "access to crucially important social, intellectual and technical skills associated with that history which could be used to resolve current problems." For this reason Wilson points out that historical amnesia can handicap the person or group suffering from it. In his "Message to the Grassroots" speech, Malcolm X explained the importance of history for problem solving: "Of all our studies, history is best qualified to reward our research. And when you see that you've got problems, all you have to do is examine the historic method used all over the world by others who have problems similar to yours. And once you see how they got theirs straight, then you know how you can get yours straight."

Wilson continues by explaining that history plays a very important role in the oppression of a people. Wilson explains:

> History is real; it brings real, tangible results. When we wish to negate it and not integrate it, when we wish to negate it and not affirm it, then it negates us in the end. The negation wins out. The Afrikan person who lives in social amnesia brought on by the projection of mythological Eurocentric history, lives a life that is unintegrated and misunderstood.

A lack of understanding of history also leads to a lack of understanding of one's own actions, as Wilson explains:

> Consequently, when the European makes us unconscious of our own history, we not only become unconscious of our history as knowledge, we become unconscious of the sources of our behavior as persons and as a people; and our own behavior becomes a mystery. "Why do Black-folks act like that?" We get discouraged.

So in studying and understanding one's history we also come to find the roots of particular problems, as well as the solutions or frameworks for developing solutions for those problems. Therefore history cannot be merely dismissed as something that happened in the past and has no real relevance to the lives of people in the present. History forms the very basis for the present and in the case of African people, history forms the very framework for which we strive towards finding solutions to the problems that we face.

The European slave masters recognized this to some extent, which is why robbing African people of their history was such a critical aspect to the process of indoctrinating the slave. This repression of history continued to be an important aspect of white supremacist domination of African people. For this reason in the British colonies African students were made to learn that Mungo Park had discovered the Niger River, despite the fact that Park had been shown to the river by Africans. In the French colonies, Africans were educated on the Gauls. Thus an African educated within the colonial system came to know more about the history of Europeans than their own history.

The indoctrination of African people with European history in the classroom takes other forms as well. Amos Wilson points out that even a subject such as math is influenced by history, which is why Africans were meant to think that math and science were created in Europe. Thus the Pythagorean theorem, Euclidean geometry, and Boolean algebra are linked to the Europeans who are credited with inventing these things, and these formulas are linked to European history. Wilson states: "We're not learning just neutral science and mathematics;

European history is inculcated right in their study." Wilson continues by stating: "In every discipline we study in college/university/school we're going to run into European history: it is intimately intertwined with all disciplines." A great example of this is the fact that the Greek physician Hippocrates is popularly known as the "Father of Medicine," when the Egyptian physician Imhotep predates Hippocrates by more than 1,000 years.

One person who recognized the importance of African history and identity was the historian Carter G. Woodson. In an attempt to integrate black history into school curriculums Woodson created Negro History Week, which eventually expanded into Black History Month. In 1976, the American government decided to officially recognize Black History Month. President Gerald Ford gave a message concerning the celebration of Black History Month, which read in part: "The last quarter-century has finally witnessed significant strides in the full integration of black people into every area of national life. In celebrating Black History Month, we can take satisfaction from this recent progress in the realization of the ideals envisioned by our Founding Fathers. But, even more than this, we can seize the opportunity to honor the too-often neglected accomplishments of black Americans in every area of endeavor throughout our history."

Right there in Ford's statement we see the distortion of history because the same Founding Fathers that Ford invokes did not in fact envision an America in which black people were integrated into "every area of national life." Many of those

Founding Fathers were slave holders. Thomas Jefferson, in particular, was convinced of the inferiority of African people. He wrote: "I advance it therefore as a suspicion only, that the blacks, whether originally a distinct race, or made distinct by time and circumstances, are inferior to the whites in the endowments of both body and mind." Therefore, if the accomplishments of black people in America are neglected, Founding Fathers like Thomas Jefferson played a major role in doing so.

The establishment of Negro History Week (which eventually would become Black History Month) has certain limitations given the structure of the American education system in which Negro History Week emerged. Malcolm X once referred to Negro History Week as a "trick." He disliked the fact that during this one week out of the whole year they decided to educate black people about their history in the United States. Moreover, the history never extends to the history of African people before slavery. Malcolm explained: "They give us the impression with Negro History Week that we were cotton pickers all of our lives. Cotton pickers, orange growers, mammies, and uncles for the white man in this country—this is our history when you talk in terms of Negro History Week." Malcolm further recognized the political and economic function of the study of history. For example, George Washington Carver was a popularly celebrated figure during Negro History Week, yet as Malcolm pointed out, Carver died in poverty and all of his inventions went towards benefitting white people such as Henry Ford. In this regard, Malcolm recognized Negro History Week as merely being a celebration of things African people achieved for their masters in the Western Hemisphere, and not the things that they have achieved on their own as freed men and women.

There is also an ego massaging aspect of the celebration of Black History Month that Amos Wilson warns us about. Wilson warns that the study of history "cannot be a mere celebration of those who struggled on our behalf" otherwise "Black History Month becomes an exercise in the inflation of egos; it becomes an exercise that cuts us further off from reality." Wilson argues instead that we should be "instructed" by history and that we should transform history "into concrete reality" and development to aid in our survival as a people.

This is why the study of African history is such a critical aspect of the development of African people. Not only is the study of history the study of certain outstanding individuals, but it is also the study of societies, cultures, economies, and political systems. In studying African civilizations African people are studying nation building techniques. Returning to Wilson's statements, the study of history is not merely an ego building exercise, but a holistic experience that is meant to inform people on a range of different issues.

Black History Month therefore cannot be the mere celebration of token black folks that enriched Europeans nor can it a mere ego massaging celebration of heroic personalities. In fact, the whole concept of a Black History Month needs to be redefined. Europeans never needed such a week or a month because their history is not only integrated into the classrooms, but it is integrated in nearly every aspect of the society. African people must also come to a point where our history is completely integrated with every aspect of our societies, much as it is in European societies.

Selected References:

Amos Wilson, *The Falsification of Afrikan Consciousness*, (Afrikan Info Systems, 1993).

Anténor Firmin, *The Equality of Human Races*

Chancellor Williams, *The Destruction of Black Civilization*, (Chicago: Third World Press, 1987).

E.A. Wallis Budge, *Osiris and the Egyptian Resurrection*, 1911.

Gerald Ford, "Message on the Observance of Black History Month," February 10, 1976.

John Gardner Wilkinson, *The Manners and Customs of the Ancient Egyptians, Volume 1*, 1883.

Marcus Garvey, "Who and What is a Negro," (1923).

W.E.B. Du Bois, *The Negro*, (New York: Holt, 1915).

William Leo Hansberry, *Pillars in Ethiopian History*, (Howard University Press, 1981).

2 AFRICAN SELF-OPPRESSION

"Africans today do not know who they are because they never studied nor tried to discover who they were yesterday. However, they have been told they are inferior to whites. Do our youths not deserve to be allowed to find out for themselves who they are? Do we not owe them the duty of providing them with an African education which allows them, to reach their own conclusions on the basis of evidences? Through Western education, we have mostly misled African youths. And we, in doing so, have inadvertently designed a hopeless future for them."
 -Sophie Oluwole

"Why, I think to teach a man to hate himself is much more criminal than teaching him to hate someone else."
-Malcolm X

S.L. Bartky (1990) explains:

> When we describe a people as oppressed, what we have in mind most often is an oppression that is economic and political in character. But recent liberation movements, the black liberation movement and the women's movement in particular, have brought to light forms of oppression that are not immediately economic or political. It is possible to be oppressed in ways that need involve neither deprivation, legal inequality, nor economic exploitation; one can be oppressed psychologically-the 'psychic alienation' of which Fanon speaks. To be psychologically oppressed is to be weighed down in your mind; it is to have a harsh dominion exercised over your self-esteem. The psychologically oppressed become their own oppressors; they come to exercise dominion over their own self-esteem. Differently put, psychological oppression can be regarded as the "internalization of intimations of inferiority."

The above quote—which references the black liberation movement—demonstrates that oppression is not merely a political or economic state, but a psychological state as well; one in which the oppressed accepts their own oppression and internalizes it. They rationalize their own oppression by accepting their inferiority. This was what was done to African people who were enslaved in the Americas. These enslaved men and women were stripped of their very humanity. They were robbed of their names and their languages. They were told that they were a people with no history, no culture, and no religion of note. They were humiliated and abused on a regular basis. This was a process through which the minds of African people were essentially destroyed.

Even after the abolition of slavery, African people have retained many of the negative behaviors and mentalities that were reinforced on the slave plantations. The result of this type of mental conditioning is that it alienates African people from themselves and makes them often act in ways that go against their own interests or that reinforce their inferiority. Na'im Akbar (1980) describes this as the alien-self disorder:

> The alien-self disorder represents that group of individuals who behave contrary to their nature and their survival. They are a group whose predominant behavior patterns represent a rejection of their natural and culturally valid dispositions. They have learned to act in contradiction to their own life and well being and as a consequence they are alienated from themselves.

Chancellor Williams (1987) also wrote of this type of self-alienation as follows:

> The present-day confused outlook of the African people is the result of centuries of Caucasian acculturation—a quite natural process wherever one people came under the economic, political and social domination of another people. The ideologies and value system of the oppressors quite unconsciously become those of the oppressed—even when the result is demonstratively against themselves.

This type of self-alienation creates a situation in which African people partake in or justify their own oppression. One example of this was Jacobus Capitein. He was an African who had formerly been enslaved by a Dutch captain. Despite having been a slave, Capitein became a defender of slavery after he was given his freedom. For Capitein the fact that slavery introduced Africans to Christianity was more important than the fact that it had robbed those very people of their own freedom and liberty. This type of conditioning was so effective that Olaudah Equiano who was born in Africa came to view Africans as "uncivilized" and accepted the supremacy of British culture and civilization, despite the hardships that Equiano suffered under slavery at the hands of Englishmen. Unlike Jacobus Capitein, Equiano was an abolitionist who argued against slavery, but it also cannot be ignored that Equiano assimilated himself into the life of an Englishman largely because of his belief that the Christian civilization of the Europeans was more civilized than that of his own African homeland.

Sadly, Equiano failed to recognize the value of his own culture. For example, he writes that "we were totally unacquainted with swearing, and all those terms of abuse and reproach which find their way so readily and copiously into the languages of more civilized people." Equiano did not question why it is that the "more civilized people" swore more than his people did. Equiano noted that his people were cleanly. He writes: "This necessary habit of decency was with us a part of religion, and therefore we had many purifications and washings; indeed almost as many, and used on the same occasions, if my recollection does not fail me, as the Jews." Equiano also explained that his people had doctors who "were very successful in healing wounds and expelling poisons." Nothing about Equiano's description of his people suggests that they were uncivilized or less civilized than Europeans.

Equiano came to view Europeans as being superior to himself and for this reason he sought to become more like them:

> I could now speak English tolerably well, and I perfectly understood every thing that was said. I now not only felt myself quite easy with these new countrymen, but relished their society and manners. I no longer looked upon them as spirits, but as men superior to us; and therefore I had the stronger desire to resemble them; to imbibe

their spirit, and imitate their manners; I therefore embraced every occasion of improvement; and every new thing that I observed I treasured up in my memory.

The oppressed African is not only oppressed by those who oppress him, but the oppressed African is also oppressed within his/her own mind. That is to say that the oppressed African often internalizes white supremacy. These Africans view everything African about themselves as being negative and subsequently uphold that which is un-African. Calypsonian and schoolteacher Hollis Liverpool (the Mighty Chalkdust) commented on how African people attempted to run away from their own heritage in his song "They Ain't See Africa At All."

I see black women

Running from their race

They own black children

They can't face

They don't know their roots

Has a glorious bloom

Blessed be the fruit of their womb

They does be acting as though

Wong (Omowale)

They shame of their history

They does be proud of other people's own

They does be glad to disclose

Their baby's ancestry

Putting their child up

On a false throne

Not their own

For hear them boast

To they friends

And they neighbor

My baby's nose

From he Spanish grandfather

My grandmother married a Chiney name Lao

That is why the eyes so pretty

And he has such thick eyebrow

He dimple come from me husband side

Whose great grandfather was Irish

And watch how the eyes pretty and wide

'Cause me mother mixed with British

Chalkdust notes with irony that no matter how dark-skinned the child is, the parents refuse to acknowledge their baby's African ancestry. In the final verse, Chalkdust mentions his neighbor. This neighbor not only boasts that she's a Yankee and refuses to wear dashikis or partake in anything that is culturally African, but Chalkdust also notes the irony in the fact that her first response when her husband leaves her is to go to the obeah man. Despite this, Chalkdust's neighbor still does not recognize Africa. Chalkdust sings: "The obeah man give she bush bath to bring back Paul/ She ain't see Africa at all."

The situation that Chalkdust notes here is that no matter how dark-skinned an African in the Caribbean is and no matter how culturally African they may be, that very African identity carries with it a stigma and as such African people attempt to escape from it. This is a very profound point which speaks to the reality that very often African people internalize notions of their own inferiority. In fact, for many the very notion of their African identity carries with it negative connotations. As such they wish to disassociate themselves from that identity and prefer not to regard themselves as Africans. Such people may make statements along the lines of

"I'm not an African, I'm black" or "I'm not an African, I'm an American."

Turning to another calypsonian, Shadow, in his song "Unite African," he points out that other groups have no problems in identifying themselves, but Africans tend not to identify as Africans:

A Chinaman is a Chinaman

A Syrian is a Syrian

An African is a Vincentian

A Jamaican

A Grenadian

Shadow continues to point out that an Indian man is an Indian man "in any land," but that the African man is a "mix up man" with no proper sense of identification. In the song Shadow urges African people to "identify" themselves as a means of uniting with each other across the Diaspora:

Chinaman helping Chinaman

Syrian helping Syrian

African making confusion

About who is American

And who is a West Indian

What Shadow is pointing out here is not only that African people have difficulties in identifying themselves as African people, but also that such a lack of understanding prevents African people from uniting and working together as other groups have done.

The Haitian scholar Jean Price-Mars also noted the negative response that he received for even daring to speak about Africa:

> I understand full well the repugnance with which I am confronted in daring to speak of Africa and African things. The subject seems vulgar to you and entirely devoid of interest, am I not right?

Even some like Frantz Fanon, who was able to accurately describe how African people internalized this racism, was himself also a victim of that same internalized racism when it came to the selection of his partners. *Black Skin, White Masks*, which was written by Frantz Fanon in 1952, is a classic study of the impact of racism on the psyche of black men and women. One of the particular ways this racism plays itself out, as Fanon points out, is that it often leads black people to seek white partners. Of black women who seek white men Fanon writes: "It is because the Negress feels inferior that she aspires to win admittance into the white world." Fanon also records meeting students from Martinique who admitted to him that "they would find it impossible to marry black men." This is because, according to Fanon, girls in Martinique know and repeat the mantra which states that the race must be whitened. For them the only way to save the race is to whiten it. Fanon observed: "It is always essential to avoid falling back into the pit of niggerhood, and every woman in the Antilles, whether in a casual flirtation or in a serious affair, is determined to select the least black of men." Not only this, but Fanon also asserts that, "It is in fact customary in Martinique to dream of a form of salvation that consists of magically turning white."

Writing from the perspective of black men who go after white women, Fanon states:

> I want to be recognized not as Black but as White [...] who better than the white woman to bring this about? By loving me she proves to me that I am worthy of a white love. I am loved like a white man. I am a white man.

Considering that Fanon himself married a white woman one can question whether or not Fanon suffered from the same self-hatred (or confusion) that he is describing in *Black Skin, White Masks*. Fanon quotes Rene Maran in stating that "mulattoes and Negroes have only one thought from the moment they land in Europe: to gratify their appetite for white women." Fanon, quoting Rene Maran again, writes that these black men "tend to marry in Europe not so much out of love as for the satisfaction of being the master of a European woman; and a certain tang of proud revenge enters into this." Fanon also adds: "Talking recently with several Antilleans, I found that the dominant concern among those arriving in France was to go to bed with a white woman."

It is a bit strange that Fanon spends so much time analyzing interracial relationships and analyzing the self-hatred or a desire for whiteness of some black people that led them to these relationships, but when it came to his own personal life Fanon saw no contradiction in his relationships with white women. Fanon here sounds very much like the mulatto women that he mentions in *Black Skin, White Masks*. These women refused to marry black men and stated as their reason for doing so: "I can choose who I want as a husband." Likewise, Fanon only pursued relationships with white women, perhaps thinking that his choice of a spouse was solely his own business.

Fanon subconsciously must have been influenced by the very concept that he wrote of; this concept that the white woman represents a type of status symbol for black men. It is indeed a curious contradiction that Fanon spent so much time denouncing internalized racism and French colonialism, when, in fact, he was deeply integrated with French values and with French women. Fanon's first child was born from a brief relationship that Fanon had with a white woman named Michelle. Fanon never married this woman and later left her and the child, which put her in the tough situation of having to raise a child on her own, while also dealing with the stigma of having given birth to a child out of wedlock. Fanon apparently had no intentions of forming a serious relationship with Michelle. This was simply Fanon gratifying his "appetite for white women." Fanon demonstrates the complex nature in which white supremacy can dominate the psyche of African people. Even those who recognize the harmful impact of internalized racism can still fall victim to certain aspects of this self-hatred.

The idea of white women representing a status symbol for African men was the subject of an article by Tânia Regina Pinto written in *Raça Brasil*. Tânia Regina Pinto mentions an interview with an unidentified black businessman, who is called DP by Pinto to hide his real identity. Pinto explains that DP married his wife solely because she was white. He confessed that in their twenty-two years of marriage they never held an intelligent conversation. At the same time, DP also admitted that he would have refused to marry a college educated black girl if he was given the opportunity. DP ultimately concluded that in marrying a white woman he saw "the gateway to a better world." Psychologist Sérgio Ferreira da Silva explains that "black men prefer blondes for fear of perpetuating the race. When you look at black, you see the dirty, the tar, the monkey. And what he experiences as a child in school he brings to his adult life. Then when he thinks of marrying, he searches for the white woman as the object of the denial of his own color." This was precisely the case with DP.

Earlier it was mentioned that Fanon wrote of how in the Antilles it was common to find black women that refused to marry black or dark-skinned men because of this idea that through "whitening" themselves they will achieve a sort of liberation. We see a similar thing playing out in the history of Brazil where historically white partners were considered more desirable. Bethan Rafferty explains:

> The idea of European aesthetic ideals remaining at the top of the Brazilian beauty hierarchy is demonstrated when mulatas also desire to 'whiten' their families; if mulattos were truly considered the most beautiful and desirable part of Brazilian society, mulatas would wish to have sexual partners who are also mulattos, however mulatas conform to the Brazilian craving for partners who are lighter than themselves.

Malcolm X once explained that the desire that some African men have for marrying European women is out of this belief that everything European symbolizes progress for African people. Malcolm explained:

> The white man has brainwashed the so-called Negro to the point of believing in white supremacy so much that today some Negroes think that they're not making progress or they don't have anything unless they're living in a white neighborhood [...]

> they don't think they are successful in life
> unless they have a white woman as a wife.

White supremacy has shaped and structured the thinking of African people in such a way that the things we strive for are often that which makes us less African and more like Europeans. The examples that were dealt with above speak to the fact that such conditioning has led many Africans to view European partners as being superior or more desirable than African partners, but there are other examples. Returning once more to Chalkdust's song, he mentions behaviors such as his neighbor refusing to wear a dashiki. In fact, it is not uncommon in the Caribbean or in Africa to find Africans who prefer European style clothing to that of traditional African clothing.

This level of self-hate is such that some of those who challenged white supremacy have not been able to completely escape the association of whiteness as representing a higher standard of development or beauty. In 1885, Anténor Firmin published *The Equality of Human Races* as a response to arguments put forward by a writer named Arthur de Gobineau on the inequality of human races. In this work, Firmin essentially dismisses the classification of human races into inferior and superior categories. Despite being a very influential work in establishing the humanity of black people and challenging white supremacy, one of the weaknesses in Firmin's work is that in attempting to challenge the purported inferiority of

African people, he is still beholden to Eurocentric standards of beauty.

Firmin states that: "We cannot deny, however, that the European's color enhances the beauty of a face better than the Ethiopian's does." Firmin continues to argue that the European does not have the best complexion, however. Firmin states: "I find it by preference, the most beautiful complexion is that of the hybrid of a Black and a White, that of the mulatto." What we can gather from this is that in Firmin's view the beauty of full-blooded Africans pales in comparison to that of Europeans and mulattos. The viewpoint Firmin expresses here seems to fall in line with the thinking that the most beautiful features in the African race come from mixing with Europeans and that Europeans generally have a better complexion than Africans do. Even more concerning is that although Firmin states that it is his preference that hybrids have the most beautiful complexion, he presents the argument that Europeans have a better complexion than African people as "the facts."

Firmin does not end his comparison of European and African beauty with just assessing complexions. Firmin also compares the beauty of faces, to which he asserts that beauty is found in white people more often than in any other race:

> The beauty of the human face has to do with the regularity of its features, which are enhanced by the purity and variety of its lines, and more particularly, by its animation

and liveliness. Thus defined, beauty admittedly may be found much more often in the White race than in the Black African race and especially in the Yellow Mongolian race.

Firmin also has much praise for a French writer named Michelet. Firmin states that Michelet's "solidarity with the Black race is most appreciated" because Michelet has "written these unforgettable golden words about Black women". The golden words are:

> I was happy to learn that in Haiti, freedom, well-being, culture, and education have caused the Negress to disappear, even when no *metissage* has occurred. She has become the Black woman, with a fine nose and thin lips; even her hair has been transformed…Even when she remains a Negress and her features have not been refined, the Black woman has a very beautiful body. […] The Black woman is an altogether different female from the proud Greek woman; she is essentially young in her blood, in her heart, and in her body, sweetly humble, childish, eager to please.

In essence, Firmin is grateful for Michelet's praise of Black women in comparison to Greek women, but he has little to say about Michelet's apparent joy over the fact that "culture and education" have caused "the Negress to disappear" and take on features that resemble Europeans. It is sadly ironic that such an argument about beauty was being put forward in a book that purports to prove, scientifically, that all of the races are equal, but this just demonstrates further how Eurocentric tastes and standards were ingrained in African people.

Africans in the Diaspora, especially, have been made to despise their African roots and therefore unwittingly made to despise themselves, as Malcolm X explained:

> They always project Africa in a negative light: jungle savages, cannibals, nothing civilized. Why then naturally it was so negative that it was negative to you and me, and you and I began to hate it. We didn't want anybody telling us anything about Africa, much less calling us Africans. In hating Africa and in hating the Africans, we ended up hating ourselves, without even realizing it. Because you can't hate the roots of a tree, and not hate the tree. You can't hate your origin and not end up hating yourself. You can't hate Africa and not hate yourself.

Of the many negative consequences of this feeling of self-hate in African people is that it kills all ambition on the part of African people. Turning once more to Malcolm X, he explained that such brainwashing had the effect of destroying the self-confidence of African people and making them constantly dependent on Europeans:

> It made us feel inferior; it made us feel inadequate; made us feel helpless. And when we fell victims to this feeling of inadequacy or inferiority or helplessness, we turned to somebody else to show us the way. We didn't have confidence in another black man to show us the way, or black people to show us the way. In those days we didn't. We didn't think a black man could do anything except play some horns—you know, make some sound and make you happy with some songs and in that way. But in serious things, where our food, clothing, shelter and education were concerned, we turned to the man. We never thought in terms of bringing these things into existence for ourselves, we never thought in terms of doing things for ourselves. Because we felt helpless.

What Malcolm was saying here was that in making African people hate themselves, Europeans made African people feel helpless. They conditioned African people to be reliant on Europeans for their very survival. Martin Delany once observed this feeling of dependency. He explained:

> Unfortunately for us, as a body, we have been taught to believe, that we must have some person to think for us, instead of thinking for

ourselves. So accustomed are we to submission and this kind of training, that it is with difficulty, even among the most intelligent of the colored people, an audience may be elicited for any purpose whatever, if the expounder is to be a colored person; and the introduction of any subject is treated with indifference, if not contempt, when the originator is a colored person. Indeed, the most ordinary white person, is almost revered, while the most qualified colored person is totally neglected. Nothing from them is appreciated.

Such a mentality of dependency stunts the development of African people. This has been one of the greatest weaknesses of those Africans who have promoted integration and assimilation as keys to uplifting African people. One such person who held this belief was an American activist named William Monroe Trotter. Trotter was such a staunch believer in integration that according to his colleague W.E.B. Du Bois, while they were students at Harvard, Trotter had white friends, but "he did not seek other colored students as companions." Trotter opposed segregation in all of its forms. As such, Du Bois noted that Trotter "would not allow a colored Y.M.C.A. in Boston, and he hated to recognize colored churches, or colored colleges." Du Bois noted that at the time of Trotter's death the segregation situation had gotten worse. Trotter refused to recognize black churches, yet Du Bois noted that there were fewer black people in Boston churches than when Trotter began his crusade against segregation. At the time of Trotter's death there was no black Y.M.C.A. and there were very few black members of the white Y.M.C.A. Trotter had spent his life fighting to achieve the integration of white institutions rather than building independent black institutions, and by the time of his death black people were in greater need of independent institutions than when Trotter started.

African people who are systematically oppressed under white supremacy find themselves in a state of "learned helplessness," in which they come to believe that the ability to change their condition lies not within their own efforts, but that their liberation is held within the power of Europeans. We not only see this among African integrationists in the United States, but also in African nations that are dependent on foreign aid from Western nations. Despite gaining independence, these Africans nations continued to be economically and psychologically dependent on the very nations that they struggled to achieve their independence from. For Thomas Sankara the greatest challenge of the revolution in Burkina Faso was the lingering influence of France colonialism:

> The greatest difficulty we have faced is the neocolonial way of thinking that exists in this country. We were colonized by a country, France, that left us with certain habits. For us, being successful in life, being

happy, meant trying to live as they do in France, like the richest of the French.

To break the chains of European psychological domination, African people must be made to see the beauty of their own culture, heritage, and physical appearance. African people must recognize how this psychological oppression plays into other forms of oppression such as political and economic oppression. We must also recognize that breaking these chains is no easy task. African self-hatred is reinforced through a number of means. One of which is through poverty. African people around the world have a lower standard of living than their European counterparts. For this reason, some Africans tend to equate Europeans with wealth and Africans with poverty. Therefore, we see that the self-hatred of African people is a psychological affliction, but one that is often rooted in material realities such as the state of poverty that African people find themselves in. As such it is natural for African people to believe that in imitating Europeans, in becoming like Europeans, they then can escape their poverty and state of oppression.

Jesse Lee Peterson, the founder of a religious organization known as the Brotherhood Organization of a New Destiny (BOND), once publicly thanked God and white people for slavery because it took blacks away from Africa. Peterson's reasoning was that Africa is so "bad" that it is a blessing for black people to have been taken out of Africa. At no point does Peterson consider that Africa's poverty was a result of European exploitation. Moreover, Peterson described the Middle Passage as being "pretty tough." This "pretty tough" voyage resulted in the deaths of numerous Africans, who died of starvation and disease. As flawed as Peterson's reasoning is some African people have in fact come to view slavery as a blessing because it took them away from Africa and brought them into Western society. Capitein, who was mentioned earlier, once proclaimed that God "led me from Africa into the blessed land of Holland […]."

We see a similar situation on the slave plantations, in which lighter-skinned slaves attempted to "pass" for white in order to achieve their freedom. In Brazil there is the famous case of Chica da Silva who became a white woman, culturally, to escape from the bondage of slavery and her children continued this cycle by attempting to rid themselves of their own African identity. As John O'Neal explained: "Racism systematically verifies itself when the slave can only break free by imitating the master: by contradicting his own reality." This is precisely what Silva and many other enslaved Africans were forced to do.

We can also go back to Olaudah Equiano who, in his quest to abolish the practice of slavery, also adopted English customs and culture. Despite the horrendous things that he endured and witnessed others endure at the hands of Europeans, Equiano later married an English woman and proudly viewed himself as an Englishman. He believed that Englishmen were superior to Africans. Moreover,

Equiano expressed a love for his first master, Michael Henry Pascal.

Pascal was an officer in the British navy and the man who gave Equiano the name Gustavus Vassa. Keep in mind that Equiano was beaten into accepting this name. Equiano served Pascal for several years and during this period of time Pascal took Equiano's wages and prize money. Despite promising to give Equiano his freedom, Pascal instead sold Equiano to a captain named James Doran, who in turn returned Equiano to the West Indies where Equiano would remain a slave until he bought his freedom. Despite his treatment at the hands of Pascal, Equiano insisted that he still loved his master, "notwithstanding his usage of me [...]."

Stockholm syndrome occurs when a captive comes to sympathize and identify with their captors. The syndrome is named after a bank robbery which occurred in Stockholm, Sweden. During the robbery a number of bank employees were held hostage for six days. During this time they bonded with their captors to the point that they saw the police as being their enemies in the situation. We see a level of Stockholm syndrome in Equiano, who was stolen from his African homeland and became attached to "old England." He identified with his captors and disassociated himself from his land of birth. Moreover, as John O'Neal noted, Equiano was a slave who believed that his freedom laid in becoming like an Englishman.

African people must make it a priority to work toward ridding ourselves of any type of inferiority complex or self-hatred. As stated before, this is no easy task due to the fact that such feelings of self-hatred are often reinforced through a number of means, the most obvious one being the fact that African people are oppressed and as such come to associate their own identity with oppression and European identity with freedom. Moreover, such a state of self-hatred has caused some Africans to even attempt to rationalize or defend their own subjugation and oppression (as we saw with Jacobus Capitein and Jesse Lee Peterson). For this reason one of the necessary steps to achieving the liberation of African people is to free African people from the bondage of psychological oppression.

Selected References:

Bethan Rafferty, "Is the high value placed on the beauty of mulatas in Brazil an example of Brazil's racial democracy or, in fact, an instance of its profound racism?"

Blake T. Hilton, "Frantz Fanon and Colonialism: A Psychology of Oppression," *Journal of Scientific Psychology*, December 2011.

Carolyn Fluehr-Lobban, "Anténor Firmin and Haiti's contribution to anthropology," *Gradhiva* 1, 2005.

Chancellor Williams, *The Destruction of Black Civilization*, (Chicago: Third World Press, 1987).

David Kofi Amponsah, "Christian Slavery, Colonialism, and Violence: The Life and Writings of an African Ex-Slave, 1717–1747," *Journal of Africana Religions*, Volume 1, Number 4, 2013, pp. 431-457

Frantz Fanon, *Black Skin, White Masks*, (Pluto Press, 2008).

H. Rap Brown, *Die Nigger Die!*, 1969.

Isaac Prilleltensky and Lev Gonick, "Polities

Change, Oppression Remains: On the Psychology and Politics of Oppression," *Political Psychology*, Vol. 17, No. 1 (Mar., 1996), pp. 127-148

Martin Delany, *The Condition, Elevation, Emigration, and Destiny of the Colored People of the United States*, 1852.

Na'im Akbar, *Akbar Papers in African Psychology*, (Mind Productions & Associates, Inc.)

Olaudah Equiano, *The Interesting Narrative of the Life of Olaudah Equiano, Or Gustavus Vassa, The African Written By Himself*, 1789.

Tânia Regina Pinto, "Why Do They Prefer Blondes?," *Raça Brasil*, October 1998.

Thomas Sankara, *Thomas Sankara Speaks: The Burkina Faso Revolution 1983–87*, (Pathfinder Press, 2007).

W.E.B. Du Bois, "William Monroe Trotter," *The Crisis*, 1934.

3 THE ROOTS OF VIOLENT SELF-DESTRUCTION

The term "violent self-destruction" is used to make a distinction between a self-destructive type of behavior and the issue of "Black-on-Black Violence" that people often casually speak about. This distinction has to be made because the issue of African self-destruction is not merely just the violence alone. This is not to say that the violence is not an issue, but the reality is that in all societies violence occurs within the social structure. There is no utopian society where crimes such as robbery, assault, and murder do not occur. Therefore, violence among African people within the African community, although a cause for concern that should not be overlooked or downplayed, is not in of itself a factor in the destabilization of African communities.

We are not merely dealing with individual cases of violence, but the type of violence that destabilizes and wrecks the African community; the type of violence that is widespread, frequent, systematic, and often times celebrated or boasted about within the African community. It is a fact that within Africa different ethnic groups fought fierce wars against each other, but those wars rarely led to the destabilization or destruction of entire societies. European slave trading in Africa did much to increase the destruction and destabilizing nature of violence among African people. Not only did the Europeans introduce weapons that were more destructive than what Africans had been fighting with, but by rewarding Africans for selling captives Europeans increased the incentive for Africans to engage in wars with each other to secure those captives.

The type of violence that we are assessing here is violence that is systematic, pervasive, destabilizing, and destructive towards the entire community and even entire nations. This violence takes forms such as gang violence, rape, mugging, murder, and even civil wars. Drug dealing, although not an act of violence in of itself, can be listed as an action which is aggressive and destructive towards the community in which such violent actions take place.

One of the ways in which we can assess and understand much of the African on African aggression is through the concept of "displaced aggression," which states that a person (or in this case a people) often act out their pent up aggression against a substitute target when they are unable to act out their aggression on the direct source of their frustrations. A popular example of this concept is the scenario in which a man who, after being mistreated by his boss, goes home and kicks his dog. The man does not usually abuse his dog, but in this situation the dog serves as a target for the man's aggression because he cannot take his aggression out on his boss for fear of being fired. The key in this example is that the man cannot act out against his boss because his boss has power over him, so the man takes out his aggression on a weaker target. Historically, African people have not typically been in a position to attack the root of their own frustrations and many of them turn those frustrations against other African people.

In his essay "Origins of Rituals and Customs in the Trinidad Carnival: African or European?" Hollis Liverpool gives an example of displaced aggression when discussing the kalenda stick fighters in Trinidad. Liverpool explains, "the kalenda seemed to represent a psychological release of tensions: frustration engendered by domination, and violent expressions of anger directed from below at the repressive white system of control and political organization that had eliminated many other African forms of expression. It seemed to be aggression turned towards themselves." These Africans, unable to take out their aggression against their oppressors, turned that violence towards each other through combating each other in stick fighting.

Another example of displaced aggression can be seen in South Africa, in which the practice of "necklacing" was used to eliminate those who were believed to have been collaborators with the apartheid government. The accused would have a rubber tire placed around their neck and then that tire would be set on fire to burn the victim to death. One notable case of this was a woman named Maki Skosana, who was wrongfully believed to have collaborated with the apartheid government. Unable to strike at the oppressive and racist whites that were in control of the apartheid system, some Africans turned their aggression against other Africans that were perceived as having collaborated with the apartheid regime.

Based on this concept of displaced aggression, we can understand violence among Africans as a form of displaced aggression. African people, being historically oppressed by Europeans, have often been unable to strike back at those Europeans and often take their aggression out against each other. We can look further than the concept of displaced aggression, however, and look at the very fact that African people live within a social system that has promoted the destruction of African people. Bobby E. Wright stated simply that "the European system has encouraged the killing of Blacks. Because Blacks have been led to believe that they are part of the psychopath's system, they simply follow the practice."

What Wright is saying here is that Africans have been socialized in a system of white supremacy that has encouraged the killing of African people. For this reason it is often those Africans who internalize the values of that white supremacist system that harm, exploit, and kill other Africans because that is what they have been socialized to do. The society itself cannot be separated from the self-destructive behaviors of African people. To demonstrate this we can look at two examples. The first of which is the historical situation of African people in the ghettoes of the United States. African people in the United States often find themselves living in degrading living conditions, which are dangerous to both the mental and physical health of those who live there.

Not only are the conditions of these ghettos dangerous to the well-being of those who live there, but the very structure of these ghettos lends themselves to the self-destructive behaviors of African people. These ghettoes are controlled not by the people who live there, but by outside forces. As a result, it is those outside forces that are the ones that control the destiny of those who live in the ghettoes. Malcolm X explained this when he pointed out:

> We don't have any boats or airplanes bringing drugs into this country. The white man brings it in. The white man brings it to Harlem. The white man makes you a drug addict. The white man then puts you in jail when he catches you using drugs.

Malcolm was essentially pointing out that the drugs that ravaged Harlem were not brought there by the people that live there. He explained that the people that live there did not even have the capability to bring drugs into their own communities. Therefore we see with African American communities that they are externally controlled and the people that live in those communities do not produce or bring in the very items that contribute to the destruction of the community.

Amos Wilson once compared the situation of African people in the ghettoes to a rat in a Skinner box who is at the mercy of the experimenter who wields control over the situation in the box. The rat is at the mercy of the experimenter who is in control of the rat's supply of food and water, and as such the experimenter is able to influence and control the behavior of the rat. Wilson argues that African Americans are analogous to the rat in this experiment and the ghettoes are analogous to the Skinner boxes. Wilson describes the situation as essentially African people being trapped in Skinner boxes in which rewards and punishments are manipulated by the Europeans who control those Skinner boxes. We certainly see this within ghettoes where African Americans have little control over the shipment of destructive substances within their own communities.

The second example is the numerous internal conflicts following independence in Africa. Like African American communities, nations such as Sierra Leone and Angola did not produce many of the weapons used in their civil wars. These weapons were bought from outside sources and bought through the sale of blood diamonds that they secured through the use of slave labor. Thus, we see that these were wars that were, in large part, funded by Western corporations because it was profitable for those corporations. So they provided Africans with the weapons that they used to maim, kill, and destroy each other. This is a trend that we see in a number of internal conflicts in post-colonial Africa. These are wars in which people are brutalized and maimed in a number of horrendous ways, and while no true winner emerges from such bloody and destructive confrontations, Western corporations manage to make profits from these conflicts.

Ultimately the accountability for such despicable atrocities is on the Africans who commit them, but we cannot look at internal conflicts in Africa without understanding how foreign powers have played a critical role in those conflicts. One of the most brutal examples we can look at is the state of the Central African Republic under the dictatorship of Jean-Bedel Bokassa. Bokassa was a child when his father was beaten to death by a French colonial officer for protesting the forced labor policies in the colony. Shortly after the death of his father, Bokassa's mother committed suicide out of grief. In this regard, Bokassa's upbringing was marked by the brutality and violence of French colonialism in Africa. Therefore, it is little wonder why Bokassa himself grew to become such a vicious and violent man.

Despite the fact that it was a French colonial officer that brutally killed his father and that France had oppressed his nation, Bokassa was a loyal servant of France. He fought in the French army during World War II. Bokassa left the army in 1961 and helped to establish a national army in the

Central African Republic. Bokassa overthrew his own cousin, David Dacko, in 1965. Bokassa, who cultivated a cult of personality around himself, used government funds to enrich himself. Bokassa held a number of properties in Europe, including a fifty-room mansion in France. While Bokassa was enriching himself from his position, the Central African Republic remained a poor, suffering, and underdeveloped nation.

The excesses of Bokassa's regime were supported by France. It was France that helped to pay for Bokassa's coronation as emperor of the Central African Republic in 1977. Altogether, the coronation cost \$22 million—money which was desperately needed in a nation with high infant mortality, widespread illiteracy, and few paved roads. Bokassa later stated that France paying for the coronation was the least they could do to repay him for his services as a soldier who fought for France. Not only was France supplying material support for Bokassa's regime, but Bokassa saw France as an inspiration for his rule. Bokassa was inspired by the example of Napoleon, whom Bokassa described as a "guide and inspiration." Bokassa was also very fond of Charles de Gaulle, whom he referred to as "Papa."

We see in a dictator like Bokassa someone whose childhood upbringing was marred by the violence of colonialism, someone who was inspired by those same colonialists that enslaved his people and murdered his father, and someone who was supported by France as he committed atrocities against his people and exploited his struggling nation's resources. Bokassa's abuses became so widespread that France eventually stepped in and overthrew him and put Dacko back in power.

There is also a cultural and historical element of this self-destructive violence that must be analyzed. This is the problem of cultural alienation that we see among many African people. That is to say that African people have been alienated from their original culture and identity, and forced to take up that of the European. We saw this a bit in Bokassa and his admiration for the French Empire. We also see this in the lyrics of many of the rappers from the 1990s. Many of the rappers of this era came of age during the crack epidemic that ravaged African American communities across the nation in the 1980s.

Some of these rappers were themselves drug dealers before becoming rappers and through their music they glamorized or romanticized this type of criminal behavior. In doing so they are also emulating European criminals such as Italian mobsters. This is why we see rappers such as Jay-Z dressing up to resemble an Italian mobster on the cover of his album *Reasonable Doubt*. The Notorious B.I.G. labeled himself the "black Frank White", in reference to a fictional mobster named Frank White. Rather than looking at their own African identities for inspiration, these rappers seek to imitate European criminals because they seek to identify with the perceived success and wealth of these criminals.

What we see in rappers that invoke Italian

identities to justify their promotion of violent behaviors is that they are essentially imitating the worst behaviors of Europeans. In his book *The Negro in the South*, Booker T. Washington observed that African Americans adopted some of the worst traits of white people. Washington stated:

> It is often said of the Negro that he is an imitative race. That, in a large degree, is true. That element has its disadvantages and it also has its advantages. Very often the Negro imitates the worst element in the white man; on the other hand I believe that the masses of our people imitate the best they find in the white man.

What Washington says about African people imitating the behaviors of the worst elements in white people is essentially what we see in the mentality of rappers and others who glorify destructive behaviors while imitating Italian mobsters. Of course, much of this imitation is largely based on the fact that African people have been conditioned to believe that there is nothing noteworthy about themselves or their own culture. Washington was a victim of this belief. Washington was also heavily influenced by Westernized thinking when it came to African history and the concept of civilization in Africa prior to the arrival of Europeans. This is evident here, in which Washington writes:

The Indian refused to submit to bondage and to learn the white man's ways. The result is that the greater portion of the American Indians have disappeared, the greater portion of those who remain are not civilized. The Negro, wiser and more enduring than the Indian, patiently endured slavery; and contact with the white man has given him a civilization vastly superior to that of the Indian.

Of course, various Indian tribes did in fact try to adopt the ways of the white man, but this did not stop them from being killed. These so-called "Five Civilized Tribes" were tribes that were considered civilized, yet all five of them had their civilizations destroyed by the same white men whom they were trying to imitate. Furthermore, the idea that black people "patiently endured slavery" is ridiculous when there were numerous slave revolts all over the Americas.

Washington imagines that both the Indian and the Negro were "in the darkest barbarism" when they met for the first time at Jamestown in 1619. Washington further writes:

Within a few months, then, after the arrival of the Negro in America, he was wearing clothes and living in a house—no inconsiderable step in the direction of morality and Christianity. True, the Negro slave had worn some kind of garment and occupied some kind of hut before he was brought to America, but he had made little progress in the improvement of his garments or in the kind of hut he inhabited.

Washington's understanding of slavery is that it was a benefit to Africans, who otherwise would have been uncivilized. This goes against the facts of the situation, however. African people actually enjoyed a better standard of living in the parts of Africa that they were taken from than they did on the slave plantations. If one does not know their history then one can be indoctrinated with another people's historical identity. In Washington's case he was complaining about African Americans adopting the behaviors of the "worst element" of white people, but he also believed that it was best for African Americans to imitate the best behaviors of white people. He did not question the need for African Americans to imitate other people in the first place.

This is what we see with many of these African criminals that destroy other African people. Many of them do not have a proper historical understanding of themselves or their situation. They have either internalized what white people have told them about themselves or internalized the very actions and behaviors of certain elements within the white community. Therefore, they will not see a contradiction between the manner in which they help to destroy their communities and the manner in which they uphold European heroes who have not contributed anything towards the advancement of African people.

In these individuals—those who murder and abuse their own people in the name of material acquisition—we see a distorted sense of identity. This is an identity constructed around materialism and one that measures success by financial gains. In this personality trait, not only does this individual judge his success by his financial wealth, but also boasts of his willingness to do whatever it takes to gain that wealth. That includes selling drugs that ruin the community or engaging in acts of violence. This type of individual is not only a threat to the very community that they live in, but are also a threat to themselves. In *Akbar Papers in African Psychology*, Na'im Akbar describes these people as suffering from "self-destructive disorders." Akbar explains:

> Victims of the *self-destructive disorders* are the most direct victims of oppression. These disorders represent the self-defeating attempts to survive in a society that systematically frustrates normal efforts for natural human growth. The pimps, pushers, prostitutes, addicts, alcoholics and psychotics and an entire array of conditions that are personally destructive to the individual and equally detrimental to the African American community, typify this group.

In describing the situation that such individuals find themselves in, Akbar explains:

> These are the individuals who have usually found the doors to legitimate self-determination blocked and out of the urgency for survival have chosen personally and socially destructive means to alleviate immediate wants such as pimping, pushing drugs, or prostituting. Black-on-black homicide and crime is an acting-out of the *self-destructive disorder*.

The final point which will be illustrated is that very often African people in the United States are encouraged to act in violent ways and rewarded for doing so, but only if that violence serves in the interest of the country. African people have been historically discouraged from using those same violent tactics in defense of their own rights and liberties. Malcolm X pointed this out, stating:

> As long as the white man sent you to Korea, you bled. He sent you to Germany, you bled. He sent you to the South Pacific to fight the Japanese, you bled. You bleed for white people, but when it comes to seeing your own churches being bombed and little black girls murdered, you haven't got any blood. You bleed when the white man says bleed; you bite when the white man says bite; and you bark when the white man says bark.

In an interview with Robert Penn, Malcolm spoke about a play that he had seen which was written by

James Baldwin. Malcolm stated: "I just saw his play, *Blues for Mr. Charlie*, which I thought was an excellent play until it ended. And if you've seen the end of it, you'll see what I mean." Malcolm continued on to explain that "the ending of it has the Negro again forgetting that a lynching has just taken place." When Penn pointed out that the play was being financed by the Ford Foundation, Malcolm explained that "the white power structure will subsidize anything that implies that Negroes should be forgiving and long-suffering."

We shall look at a specific example of David Fagen, who fought for America during the Philippine-American War from 1899 to 1902. Fagen was among the many black soldiers who were praised for their bravery and conduct during the Cuban War in 1898, but this did not spare them the racial insults of whites when they returned back home. In one instance, Private George Washington, who was a member of Fagen's regiment, was slashed with a razor by a white soldier after he had objected to a racial slur that the white soldier hurled at him.

Such acts of discrimination towards African Americans continued into the Filipino war. One African American who enlisted in the war was outraged when a general stated that "the Filipinos are naturally more intelligent than our colored people." In the Philippines, Fagen experienced difficulties of his own with his superiors. On November 17, 1899, Fagen snuck into the jungle. Fagen eventually joined the natives and engaged in a guerrilla war campaign against the American troops. During several encounters with his former allies, Fagen managed to evade capture, which was something that frustrated Col. Frederick Funston. There were rumors that Fagen brutally tortured and killed captive American soldiers, although many of the soldiers that were captured by him dismissed these rumors.

The resentment towards black defectors in this war was such that of the twenty soldiers who were captured for treason, the only two that were executed were black people. The order to execute them was approved by President Theodore Roosevelt, who commuted the death sentences of the other defectors. Among these black defectors, Fagen remained a constant frustration to the American forces. Fagen was never captured and his fate is unknown. George Knox summed Fagen up as follows:

> Fagen was a traitor, and died a traitor's death, but he was a man, no doubt, prompted by honest motives to help a weaker side, and one to which he felt allied by ties that bind. Fagen, perhaps, did not appreciate the magnitude of the crime of aiding the enemy to shoot down his flag. He saw, it may be, the weak, the strong, he chose, and the world knows the rest.

Although Fagen's motivations for siding with the Filipinos against America is unclear, it must have been influenced not only by the injustices that were inflicted on African people in the United States, but also by the injustices that Americans had been inflicting on the Filipinos throughout the war. The allegations of Fagen's brutalities are in doubt, but what cannot be denied is the brutal manner in which the American forces treated the Filipino people. Had Fagen fought on the side of the Americans and partook in such atrocities he may have been recorded as an American hero in the war.

Fagen was merely acting out frustrations which African Americans have felt throughout the military history of the United States. We see examples in World War II in which captive German soldiers were given better treatment than African American soldiers. In one instance, black soldiers were made to eat in segregated facilities, while the German prisoners of war ate in the main section of the diner. Despite the favorable treatment that was given to Germans, African Americans were convinced that it was in their own interest to act violently in defense of the United States, the same country which was at the same time lynching and oppressing African people. This is why Muhammad Ali refused to go to Vietnam and was sentenced for his refusal. Ali's mentor and religious leader, Elijah Muhammad, had gone to jail during World War II for similar reasons.

This is not just related to African Americans, but to African people as a whole. There were Africans that fought on the side of the British during the American Revolutionary War, yet their doing so did not change the attitude of the British towards slavery in their colonies. There were Africans from the continent that fought for the Europeans during the World Wars. These Africans were colonized and oppressed in their own lands, yet they were fighting and dying for the very nations that were oppressing them. The British were outraged over the treatment of Jews at the hands of the Nazis in concentration camps, yet no objections were raised by the British about the concentration camps they had established in Kenya.

The point that should be understood here is that white supremacy has historically rewarded African people for acting violently in defense of the interests of Europeans, but punished African people for doing the same thing in defense of their own liberty. As H. Rap Brown explained: "They send us to Vietnam and brag about what good fighters we are. It's legitimate for a Black man to go over there and kill 30 Vietcong and get a medal, but you come back here and kill one racist, red-necked, honky, camel-breathed peckerwood who's been misusing you and your people all your life and that's murder. That's homicide, because the white man has the power to define and legitimatize his actions. He can legitimatize violence. At this point we must address ourselves to defensive measures, something that will counteract that violence." This is why Thomas Jefferson was one of the Founding Fathers of the United States for his role in the American Revolution, yet this same Jefferson (who was a slave owner) condemned Haiti's revolution because it went against the self-interests of the European slave owners. Just as Americans had done, Haitians rose up in violent revolution in defense of their liberty, but this was not welcomed by the United States, who feared the implications of a successful slave uprising. This is why we must seriously consider Wright's point that African people kill each other because they have been trained within a system that has rewarded the death and destruction of African people.

Notes:

For more information on David Fagen see "David Fagen: An Afro-American Rebel in the Philippines, 1899-1901" by Michael C. Robinson and Frank N. Schubert in *Pacific Historical Review*, Vol. 44, No. 1 (Feb., 1975), pp. 68-83

4 MALADAPTIVE EDUCATION

"We have a school system that is based upon the psychology of White children and White people. We are trying to educate our children in that system; they are bound to fail. The very structure of the educational system itself is based upon a White model and therefore it has a built-in failure mechanism for us, one way or the other."
-Amos Wilson

Carter G. Woodson was among one of the earliest writers to document the impact of the miseducation of African people in his work *The Mis-Education of the Negro* (1933). In this book, Woodson noted that "Negroes are taught to admire the Hebrew, the Greek, the Latin and the Teuton and to despise the African." Woodson further explains:

> When a Negro has finished his education in our schools, then, he has been equipped to

begin the life of an Americanized or Europeanized white man, but before he steps from the threshold of his alma mater he is told by his teachers that he must go back to his own people from whom he has been estranged by a vision of ideals which in his disillusionment he will realize that he cannot attain.

Woodson's essential argument in this book is that African people go to schools which alienate them from their own identity and condition them to be imitations of their European counterparts, which effectively alienates such educated Africans from their own people. Moreover, these educated Africans are then frustrated with the fact that certain barriers exist which prevent them from truly being Europeans, despite being trained to think and act as Europeans. Woodson also argues that before African people are physically lynched, they are mentally lynched in classrooms that help to reinforce their inferiority. Woodson considered the lynching that took place in the classroom to be the "worst sort of lynching" because it "kills one's aspirations and dooms him to vagabondage and crime."

Psychologists Kenneth Clark and Mamie Clark played a seminal role in the *Brown v. Board of Education* ruling which deemed segregated education to be unconstitutional. The Clarks conducted a test in which they had black children choose between a black doll and white doll. What they found was that the majority of black children preferred the white dolls. This test provided evidence that segregated education had a detrimental impact on the self-esteem of black children and this discovery played a seminal role in the decision by the Supreme Court to overturn segregation in schools. Forty years later when the doll test was repeated, the results were the same. Clark described the results as being "disturbing."

When the same test was conducted in Trinidad and Tobago it was shown that black children had an even stronger preference for the white dolls than did children in the United States. Elmo Gopaul, the secretary general of the Trinidad and Tobago teacher's union, responded by saying: "Even in Trinidad, where 85 percent of the people are black and we have a black government, we have not recovered from 400 years in which blacks knew the white man as the boss." So it is clear that the problem remained long after segregation in schools was ruled unconstitutional, and the issue even exists in nations where African people have never experienced segregated education. The implications of Clark's study were clear, but what was the solution to this problem? Clark's findings played a major role in the *Brown v. Board of Education* case, in which segregated schools were ruled uncon-stitutional, but tests afterwards have shown repeatedly that little progress has been made in terms of improving the self-esteem of black children.

So why is it that integrated schools were not the

solution? The answer to this question lies in the fact that integration really does not get to the root of the self-esteem issues that face African children. Psychologist Asa G. Hilliard III (1978) explained:

> It must be remembered that the present push for "integrated education" had its roots in the general, belief that the education which most white children were getting was a quality education, *and* that if only Afro-American and other cultural groups could be present when this quality education was offered, they would be better off than under segregation.

The point that Hilliard was making here is that the fundamental mistake in the desegregation process was the idea that the education white people were receiving was superior. Therefore, the conclusion some came to was that by simply giving black children the same education it would improve their situation. Those who view the mere integration of schools as being a solution to the self-esteem issues of black children ignore the fact that black children did not face the same challenges that white children did, therefore they should not receive the same education. The doll test is a perfect example of this. If the black child was made to associate blackness with being ugly or unattractive, then the education that black children received should have been an education that would correct those distorted views, but no such education is to be found in the curriculum that white children received.

Rather than integrated education which taught African children the same thing that white children learned, African children should have been getting an African-centered education based on their own needs and historical experiences. It was mentioned earlier that when Clark's doll tests were conducted in Trinidad it produced similar results as in the United States, despite the fact that the government at the time was a black one. The reason for this can be found in the education that children in the Caribbean receive. Trinidadian born teacher and calypsonian Hollis Liverpool (1994) stated of the educational system in the British West Indies:

> Sad to say, too, students in the British Caribbean, especially those in history or music, know very little of the history of their music or of Latin American or even Afro-American history. Except for a few courses on Caribbean, African, and Latin American history and heritage available at the University of the West Indies, the culture of Africans in the wider African continuum (the Western Hemisphere, Africa, and Europe) is simply not taught. Yet the same students are exposed daily to European culture. Students in the U.S. Virgin Islands are better off, for at least they are exposed to U.S. and Afro-American history, but even that is limited. How then can Africans in the continuum appreciate and respect one another, or even learn of each other's

existence?

What Liverpool is describing here is essentially the same education system that prevailed during the days of British colonial rule, in which West Indians were educated to become loyal British subjects. That system of education remained entrenched in the Caribbean even after independence was achieved. The issue in the educational system of the post-colonial Caribbean is that even after Africans gained political independence from Britain, the colonial education system remained and continued to have an adverse impact on the self-image of African children.

Thus we see a parallel between the educations of Africans in the Caribbean with that of Africans in the United States. In both cases African people managed to gain more political freedoms. Caribbean nations became independent and were free to develop themselves as they saw fit, but were unable to break away from Eurocentric models of education and governance because that is what they were educated—or rather trained—to do. In the United States the successes of the civil rights movement also did not address the miseducation that African Americans underwent. The failure of integrated education was the failure to break with this Eurocentric mentality.

We also see a similar phenomenon in Nigeria, which like Trinidad, was a former British colony. The Nigerian novelist Chinua Achebe recalled that one day his four year old daughter claimed, "I am not black; I am brown." Achebe decided to investigate where his daughter had acquired such a negative perception of being black and he discovered that the books that she had been reading were books that were imported from Europe. Such books depicted Africans in demeaning ways. This urged Achebe to begin writing children's books. The point here is that even in post-colonial Nigeria, African children were faced with negative depictions of African people on a regular basis. It is also worth noting here that Achebe's daughter was not being influenced by what she was learning in school, but through the European imported books that she was reading. This demonstrates that the struggle to educate African children is one that not only takes place in the classroom, but outside the classroom as well.

Marcus Garvey once declared: "Education is not so much the school that one has passed through, but the use one makes of that which he has learned." This is relevant in light of the fact that education has often been used as a tool against African people, and a tool used to alienate African people from possessing a strong sense of self. In other words, the "education" African people have received has been typically used in order to aid in the continuing exploitation of Africans. For this reason African people have to reassess our very concept and understanding of precisely what education is.

The contradiction that we often see with education is that the educated African is not educated to benefit the African community, but they are educated rather to maintain the oppression of African people or as Bobby E. Wright (1984) explained, "Black intellectual enlightenment does not always lead to genuine insight and it can be very damaging to the intellect as reflected by the behavior of many eminent Black scientists." What is even more problematic for African people is that it is often the mis-educated Africans who occupy leadership positions within the community, but their very education renders them ineffective as leaders of African people. In *Black Power*, by Kwame Ture and Charles Hamilton (1967), we are told about the educated black leadership in the United States:

> There has developed in this country an entire class of "captive leaders" in the black communities. These are black people with certain technical and administrative skills who could provide useful leadership roles in the black communities but do not because they have become beholden to the white power structure.

Therefore what we need is not so much education, but a particular type of education that will work to the benefit of African people. In the context of educating African children, the study of history is important for the mere fact that it provides a model for education. African people were not a people without a system of education or no desire for education. In fact, Walter Rodney (1969) tells us about the demand for books in Timbuktu:

In a city which was renowned for its trade in gold, there was more profit to be made from books than from any other line of business! In other words, learning was valued more highly than gold!

For the purposes of this topic, we will look briefly at how education functioned in Africa prior to European conquest. Prior to European colonization, African societies did have their own educational systems and these educational systems were part of the function of the society. The Yoruba, for example, viewed education as a lifelong process, and not something that was over when one graduated from school. Indeed, the African concept of education was that the person is constantly growing and constantly learning. Sharon Adetutu Omotoso (2010) states that the educated person in Africa is:

> One who is equipped to handle successfully the problems of living in an immediate and an extended family; who is well versed in the folk-lores and genealogies of the ancestors; who has some skills to handle minor health problems and where to obtain advice and help in major ones; who stands well with the ancestral spirits of the family and knows how to observe their worship; who has the ability to discharge social and political duties; who is wise and shrewd in judgement; who expresses self not in too

many words but rather in proverbs and analogies leaving hearers to unravel his or her thought; who is self controlled under provocation, dignified in sorrow and restrained in success; and finally and most importantly, who is of excellent character.

Omotoso further states that: "While the Western conception of education is individualistic, the African conception of education is holistic; socially and functionally oriented. Both orientations have varying value. On a daily basis, Western individuality is eating deep into African societies; for instance, in recent marriages, communalism becomes a vice and the 'me and my wife syndrome' is raised above the traditional African communalistic style which used to exist." John K. Marah (2006) writes of the wisdom and knowledge that the griot possessed, stating:

In West Africa, there were griots 'walking dictionaries,' historians, or verbal artists who memorized the history, legends of a whole people and would recite them and teach their apprentices or audiences, publicly or privately; direct instruction was also employed.

Contributing to the holistic and community oriented feature of African education was a concept known as age-grades. Chancellor Williams (1987) described age grades as follows:

> Age grades, sets, and classes are social, economic, political, and military systems for (1) basic and advanced traditional education (formal). (2) Individual and group responsibility roles. (3) Police and military training. (4) Division of labor. (5) Rites of passage and social activities. In chiefless societies the age grades are the organs of social, economic and political action.

Education in Africa was organized in a system of age grades, and what one learned was directly linked to which level of the age grade one belonged to. Children learned the basic necessities needed to deal with the challenges of society; which included being able to name certain plants and animals. As they grew older, they were given more specialized knowledge. This education was not only divided on age, but also on gender, thus young girls got a type of education that would prepare them for womanhood. They were trained in childcare, cooking, social relations, and how to be successful wives and maintain an intimate relationship with their husbands.

We find that within African societies boys were educated in preparation for manhood and girls were educated in preparation for womanhood. This education was done through initiation societies. In Sierra Leone and Liberia, for example, there was the Poro society for boys and the Sande society for girls, which prepared boys and girls for adulthood. In *The Dark Child* (1945), Camara Laye describes the experience of being initiated in the bush schools of Guinea, stating:

> The teaching we received in the bush, far from all prying eyes, had nothing very mysterious about it; nothing, I think, that was not fit for ears other than our own. These lessons, the same as had been taught to all who had preceded us, confined themselves to outlining what a man's conduct should be: we were to be absolutely straightforward, to cultivate all the virtues that go to make an honest man, to fulfill our duties toward God, toward our parents, our superiors and our neighbors. We must tell nothing of what we learned, either to women or to the uninitiated; neither were we to reveal any of the secret rites or circumcision. That is the custom. Women, too, are not allowed to tell anything about the rites of excision.

The society trained these children in preparation to function within the social order, including the family structure. It prepared them for adulthood and for life in the societies that they would grow up to live in. Breaking up the education into age grades was also a particularly useful way to acculturate these children by gradually preparing them for adulthood, but the age grade also served another function. David Conrad (2010) explains:

One of the main purposes of age grades is to provide a sense of social togetherness that goes beyond the family. This is why, when a Mande person who is away from home meets another Mande, she or he will introduce a fellow villager as a brother or sister.

The communal and holistic nature of education in African societies provides African children with advantages that children in Western societies do not demonstrate. Marcelle Geber noticed this when she tested three hundred babies in Uganda. She found that the infants there were superior to Western children when it came to psychological maturity, coordination, and language skills. Interestingly, Geber found that children of more educated parents were less mature than the babies of mothers that were uneducated. The key difference was that the uneducated mother had a stronger attachment to the child. Therefore, it is the family orientated and communal elements of traditional African society that contributed to the development of children to the point that they matured quicker than children living in more developed countries in the Western world.

This communal approach to education differs greatly with the more individual approach of Western education. One of the problems that we see pertaining to African people in the Western system of education is the failure to recognize the societal factors that also impact the lives of African children. It is as if African children are educated in a vacuum that is removed from the daily realities of racism, oppression, self-hate, and poverty. Instead, the educational system is often geared towards finding problems that are believed to be inherent within the African child, without also assessing problems within the social structure in which those African children live. Asa G. Hilliard points out:

> The real problem of racism and oppression in education is hidden too in the popular scholarship on the problem. Almost universally, scholarly studies of educational problems for minorities focus on the search for some deficit in the minority population, which will obviously require help from those who are "qualified to help." Almost totally absent from the theories and the practical work of scholars is any study of the dynamics and mechanics of racism and oppression.

In other words, the analysis of the problem of education for African children now moves away from the source of the struggles of African children and moves towards trying to find a deficit in their character or behavior. Thus the black child's behaviors are analyzed and scrutinized, and no attention is paid to the society in which that child lives and how the society itself shapes certain behaviors. This is not only a problem within the education system, but it is a problem that confronts psychology as a whole for when analyzing social problems some have made the mistake of focusing solely on the individual while neglecting the society that the individual lives in. For example, an American sociologist named William Graham Sumner argued that poor people are poor because of their own shiftless nature. Such an analysis can only be made in a society which fails to resolve poverty. Poverty is not merely an individual issue, but is in fact largely a product of the society. This is why Walter Rodney (1969) could point out that in African societies one did not find the "extremes of poverty and abandonment which one finds in richer and supposedly more mature societies."

Amos Wilson concludes:

> Since the individual does not succeed or fail in a vacuum but succeeds or fails in a social system, the social system must be taken into consideration when we evaluate individual success and failure. This implies the possibility that the social structure itself may be principally responsible for the success of some and the failures of others.

The point Wilson makes here is that ultimately we cannot speak of the success or failure of a particular individual without taking into consideration the social structure that they live in and the societal factors that they confront on a daily basis. One of the features of the maladaptive education that African people receive is that the education very rarely confronts the realities that they are faced with. African people cannot be educated out-of-step with the daily realities they must face living in a white supremacy orientated social system.

Education in African societies was geared towards maintaining those societies and was extremely relevant to the needs of those societies. An example of this was among the Bemba people in Zambia. By the age of six a Bemba child could name up to sixty species of tree plants because tree production was relevant to this society, which used cut and burn agriculture. Among the Tiriki people, a boy had to undergo the initiation to manhood through a process that lasted about six months. In this initiation process young boys were instilled with a sense of respect for the elders and a sense of brotherhood for members of the same age set. This gave them an understanding of their own society. As Basil Davidson (1969) explains: "The Tiriki social charter is thus explained and then enshrined at the center of the man's life." The colonial education that was later introduced was not very relevant to the lives of the Africans. It served more or less to make Africans think as Europeans, thus making Africans easier to exploit. This was education that served the exploiter rather than the exploited.

Walter Rodney (1972) stated of African education:

> Indeed, the most crucial aspect of pre-colonial African education was its *relevance* to Africans, in sharp contrast with what was

later introduced. The following features of indigenous African education can be considered outstanding: its close links with social life, both in a material and spiritual sense; its collective nature; its many-sidedness; and its progressive development in conformity with the successive stages of physical, emotional, and mental development of the child. There was no separation of education and productive activity or any division between manual and intellectual education. Altogether, through mainly informal means, pre-colonial African education matched the realities of pre-colonial African society and produced well-rounded personalities to fit into that society.

Of colonial schools, Rodney states that it "was education for subordination, exploitation; the creation of mental confusion and the development of underdevelopment." This is precisely what the education that African people receive is. It is education for subordination, education that reinforces the inferiority of African people and the superiority of Europeans. The examples of African educational systems were mentioned to contrast the holistic approach that Africans had towards education with that of the European system, which has educated African people to maintain their state of being oppressed. Walter Rodney explained the reason for this type of education when he wrote: "Europeans knew well enough that if they did not control the minds of Africans, they would soon cease to control the people physically and politically."

An African centered approach to education does not judge education solely based on what degree one has or from which school one graduated from, but, as Garvey said, one must also judge education by what one does with that education. The paradox with education is that very often those who are able to make the greatest contribution to African people are the ones who do not have a great deal of formal education. Unlike his critic W.E.B. Du Bois, Garvey did not have a Ph. D. from a prestigious university like Harvard, yet he was able to accomplish more in terms of organizing and employing African people than Du Bois was able to do.

References:

Amos Wilson, *The Falsification of Afrikan Consciousness*, (Afrikan Info Systems, 1993).

Asa G. Hilliard, "Straight Talk about School Desegregation Problems," *Theory into Practice*, Vol. 17, No. 2, Desegregation: Problems and Practices (Apr.,1978), pp. 100-106

Bobby E. Wright, *The Psychopathic Racial Personality and Other Essays*, (Third World Press, 1984).

Carter G. Woodson, *The Mis-Education of the Negro*, 1933.

Chinua Achebe, "The Education of a British-Protected Child," excerpt from *New York Times*, December 15, 2009.

Daniel Goleman, "Black Child's Self-View is Still Low, Study Finds, "*New York Times*, August 31, 1987.

David Conrad, *Empires of Medieval West Africa*, (Chelsea House, 2010).

Hollis Liverpool, "Researching Steelband and Calypso Music in the British Caribbean and the U. S. Virgin Islands," *Black Music Research Journal*, Vol. 14, No. 2 (Autumn, 1994), pp. 179-20

John K. Marah, "The Virtues and Challenges in Traditional African Education," *The Journal of Pan African Studies*, vol. 1, no. 4, June 2006.

Raymond S. Moore, "Research and Common Sense: Therapies for Our Homes and Schools," *Teachers College Record*, Volume 84 Number 2, 1982, p. 355-377

Sharon Adetutu Omotoso, "Education and Emancipation: An African Philosophical Perspective," *The Journal of Pan African Studies*, vol. 3, no.9, June-July 2010.

Kwame Ture and Charles Hamilton, *Black Power: The Politics of Liberation in America*, (Random House, 1967).

Walter Rodney, *How Europe Underdeveloped Africa*, (Bogle-L'Ouverture Publications, 1972).

___*The Groundings with my Brothers*, (Frontline Distribution International, 1969).